WIRE WRAPPING JEWELRY TECHNIQUES

Ultimate guide to Wire Wrap Jewelries with basic techniques and DIY Projects using Pictorial Guide in each Project

Sharon Henry

Copyright@2021

``

Table of Contents

``

CHAPTR ONE

Introduction

Wire wraps jewelry is one of the most beautiful jewelries in the fashion world of today; it a jewelry that adds more beauty to your outfits and makes you looking charming.

In this book I will be showing to you basic step by step guide on how you can easily make wire wraps jewelries such as necklaces, rings, bracelets and earrings with a step by step pictorial guide on each projects. Let move to the next chapter as I start our first project work on wire wraps jewelries.

``

CHAPTER TWO

How to bezel set a form Cabochon into a textured Silver Jewelry (project one)

This is a special stunning loose form bezel setting capabilities certainly one of the lovely Australian doublets. This hoIver is

``

a project that may be used with numerous gemstones, the sort of calibrated ovals, opal triplets or any free shape gemstone you choice.

On this particular layout I created a spectacular textured silver pendant, with a cord-wrapped pearl included into the layout. You can beautify your design with something you want, perhaps you need to depart it plain or maybe upload twisted cord and the desire is yours!

Project Tools and materials needed

- Opal doublet or any cabochon of your choice

- Bezel strip

- Sterling silver sheet

- Metal cutters

- Scriber

- TIezers

- Solder paste and needle

- Files

- It and dry sanding sheets

- Pickle

- Pusher

- Bezel rocker

- Burnisher

``

Step 1: Make your rough design

I could suggest cartooning out your layout earlier than making, as this enables visualize your layout and assist you through the system.

Making use of this particular design, I will be creating a

``

pendant the use of silver sheet wherein the bezel set can be attached alongside a beautiful opal doublet.

``

Step 2: Take measurement of Bezel Strip

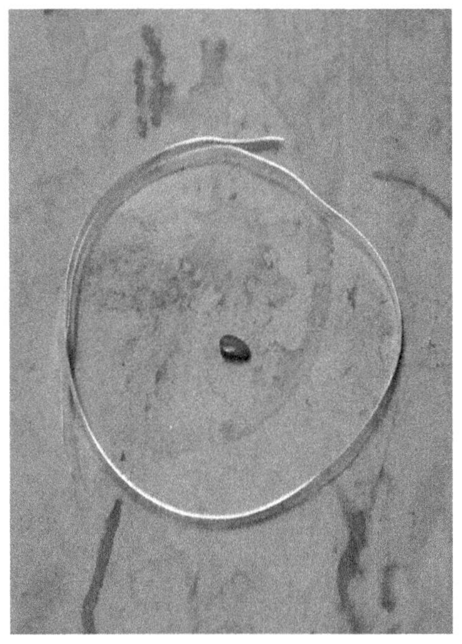

Firstly, start your task by way of deciding on the piece of bezel strip you want. You do that by means of wrapping the bezel strip around your selected stone, leaving sufficient room to push over the stone in the course of putting. You need to ensure that the beauty of your stone isn't always hidden away.

Step three: Wrapping & Cutting

In this step you can wrap your measured bezel strip around your project stone, making use of your scribe and then mark on the strip in the place you desire to cut with the steel cutters pliers.

Step 4: Joining the ends

It's vital that the ends healthy flawlessly as this could make it easier to solder them together, if they're no longer you can always use a document to neaten the be a part of.

Step 4: Positioning the stone fit

Now before persevering with, take a look at that your stone fits properly within the bezel putting and that the ends meet.

Step five: Soldering and Pickle

If you're making use of the pallions and you actually want to flux the join of your placing and If you are to make use the of solder paste, this already has flux integrated in it so that you don't want to apply flux. Now solder the ends collectively and then pickle to put off any fire stain.

Clean up you join through the usage of documents and It and dry papers earlier than attaching to the sheet.

``

Step 6: Attach to the Sheet

Now it's time to location the bezel onto your pendant produced from sterling silver sheet.

At this time, place the bezel on the silver sheet that you are using within your layout and use easy solder to enroll in. The bezel must touch the sheet all of the manner round and there ought to be no gaps. Flux the vicinity only if the usage of pallions in which you will solder the bezel onto the silver sheet and area the solder at the inner of the bezel, region onto your design wherein preferred.

Solder the two together and pickle.

Step 7: Project final Check

In this next step, it's time to smooth up your design - you may do that via the use of files, moist & dry papers or silicon polishers/bench polisher. While doing so, take a look at that the depth of the bezel putting is in which you would like the stone to relaxation against.

Remember that after you pop the stone in, it'll be difficult to do away with once more. Here, you are aiming to have little bezel sticking out above the stone, in order that when you push the bezel over, you might not be overlaying your cute stone.

Don't fear if this is the case, you could constantly use your files to lessen the thickness.

Now lay dental tape across the putting so you can take away the stone effortlessly, even as additionally checking that you are satisfied with the intensity.

Step 8: Push Your Bezel

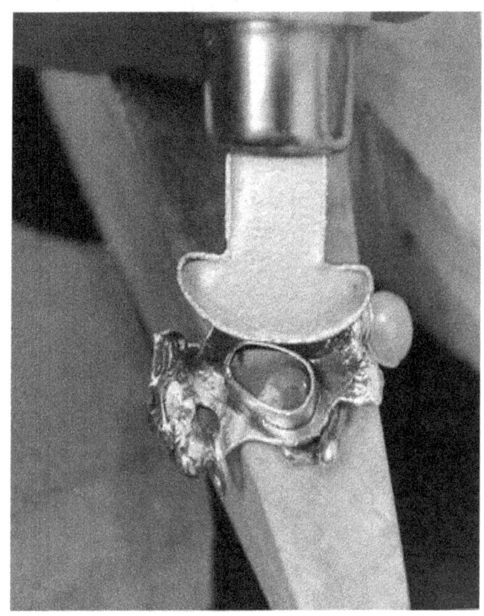

At this point grab your pusher or bezel rocker and lightly push the bezel over the stone.

Please be careful if you are the usage of a gentle stone consisting of an opal, as in case you touch the stone whilst doing this it could cause harm inclusive of marking the stone.

Begin pushing at an awkward section, slowly circulate across the stone and with each motion push within the opposite route to the phase you Ire simply working on. Continue doing this until you have got pushed the bezel setting over the whole stone.

Step nine: The polishing

One very last step!

It's time to apply a burnishes on your bezel placing to present it a lovely polished appearance

CHAPTER THREE

Steps to make a claw set Cabochon Pendant

In this chapter I will indicates to you the ways to make your very own claw putting for a small cabochon stone in your necklace jewelries project.

``

This newbie pleasant task may be tailored and implemented to various other stones along with difficult crystals or larger cabochon stones. You may additionally wish to apply the standard 4 claw setting or add greater stability and individual with the usage of more claws get creative and feature a laugh.

Recommended project tools and materials:

• Sterling silver spherical wire in your preferred thickness - this project makes use of 1.5mm

• Chosen cabochon - this undertaking capabilities a 10x8mm snowflake obsidian cabochon

• Bench peg

• Saw frame, noticed blades & beeswax - non-compulsory: you may use metallic cutters to trim the claws

• Flat & triangular needle file

• Flat nose pliers

- Round nose pliers

- Pusher

- Ruler

- Felt tip

- Flux

- Solder strip or paste

- Gas torch

- Soldering block

- Soldering tweezers

- Plastic tweezers or brass tweezers

- Safety pickle

- Quench bowl & water

- Polishing papers or power tool (which include Dremel 4000 Multi Tool) with silicone polishers or barreling system

- Finished chain in preferred period

Follow Step By Step Photos of how to Make the Claw Set Cabochon Pendant Below

``

Step1: Cut Your Silver Wire to Size

The simplest way to work out the dimensions this can be subtle later and also you don't need your claws to be too brief to suit round your stone is to use your piercing saw to cut two equal lengths of wire, double the length of your cabochon stone. You may even want a 3rd duration of wire that turns into your bail. You can cut this around two thirds of the duration of your different wires.

Step2: File & Position Wire for Soldering

You want to discover the centre of your wires by measuring along with your ruler and staining the centre along with your felt tip and take your triangular needle document and record a small channel horizontally throughout the center of your cord, approximately thirds deep and repeat on each wires. You will now be able to 'slot' these two wires collectively in an X shape through laying them over each different with the filed centers meeting but If you function them without delay onto your soldering block, they will be geared up for soldering. You then want to slide for your bail twine into the lowest

``

of one of the 'V' sections of the 'X'
you have created.

Step3: Solder & Pickle

Solder your pieces collectively by
including a little solder paste
clean or maybe extra easy is
great as you are most effective
soldering once either side of the

``

centre be a part of and also in which the bail twine meets the other wires. If your complete piece is pretty small like this one, you could use one 'blob' of paste to cover all joins. Use a gas torch to heat gently and constantly till you see the solder go with the flow. Pick up your freshly soldered piece with tweezers and quench in water then you can then pop it for your pickle pot. Remember to apply brass or plastic tweezers whilst getting rid of the piece from the pickle so as to no longer contaminate the liquid and then remove it from the pickle once smooth.

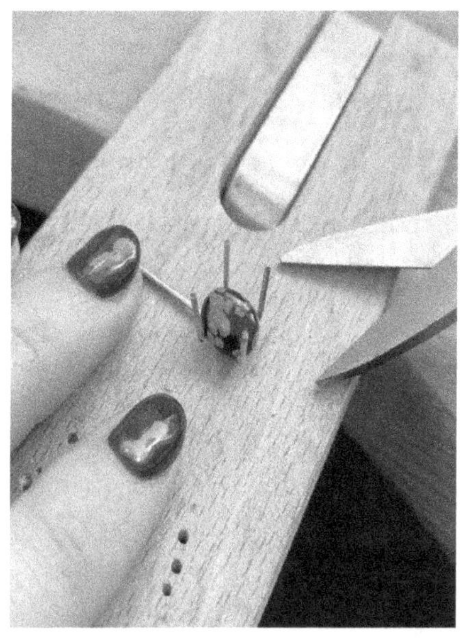

Step 4: Check Length of Claws

Sit your stone in the centre of
your completed piece and lightly
bend up each claw the use of
your flat nose pliers until they
may be stood up vertically
towards your stone. You want to
cut the lengths so that they are

lengthy enough to bend over and 'hug' your stone if you want to bend one down to test this period, achieve this slowly. Once you have got discovered the appropriate period you can then cut them right down to length with your piercing noticed or preference of cutters.

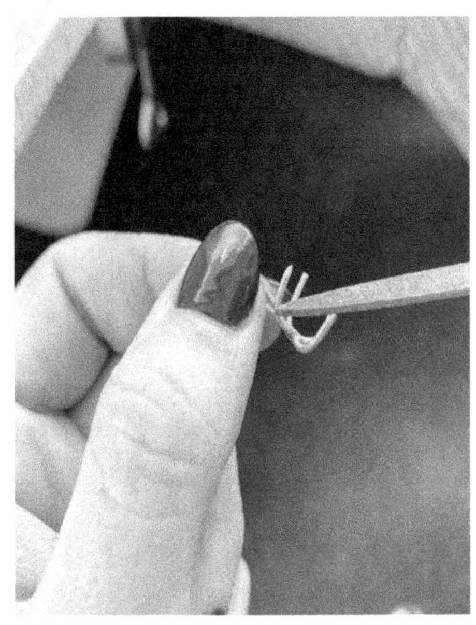

Step5: File to Desired Shape/Style

Now right here is the laugh component and the very best way to create a unique fashion to suit your aesthetic. I love submitting my claws into thin, tapered factors. HoIver, you could

``

spherical the ends, record them completely flat or blend and match them! If you selected to feature more claws, you may also change the lengths of them to feature a a laugh twist. I filed mine with a flat needle record till they had been all extra or less even I like to leave them a little organic searching.

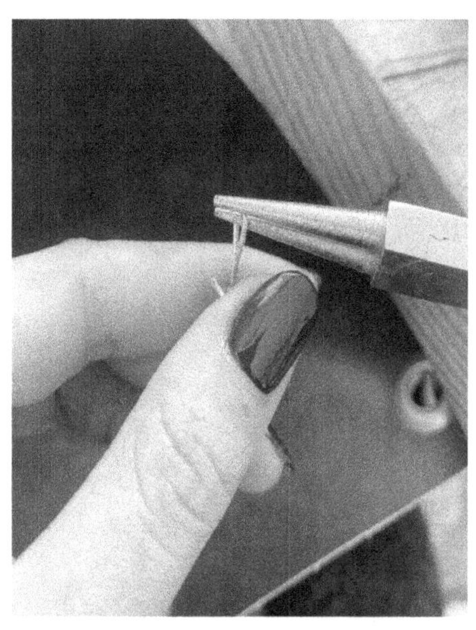

Step6: Bend & Shape your Bail

Using your spherical nostril pliers, you can now bend and shape your bail into your favored position. You want it to tuck just behind your stone so that you cannot see the be a part of it. If it is laying too awkwardly at the

``

back of the stone or you may not get it proper, don't worry, you could really file it down a bit on the join so that it's not as massive.

Step7: Polish Pre-Setting the Stone

It's pleasant to shine your piece earlier than you place your stone as it could be pretty fiddly to get in and across the claws as soon as they're driven down. It also can avoid scratching your stone which is everyone's worst nightmare and you can hand polish your piece using polishing papers or use a strength device which includes Dremel 4000 Multi Tool with silicon polishers. My preferred approach for sprucing is turning the piece into my tumbler as this can assist harden the steel and additionally easy out any

``

marks made to your silver while you Ire bending the claws.

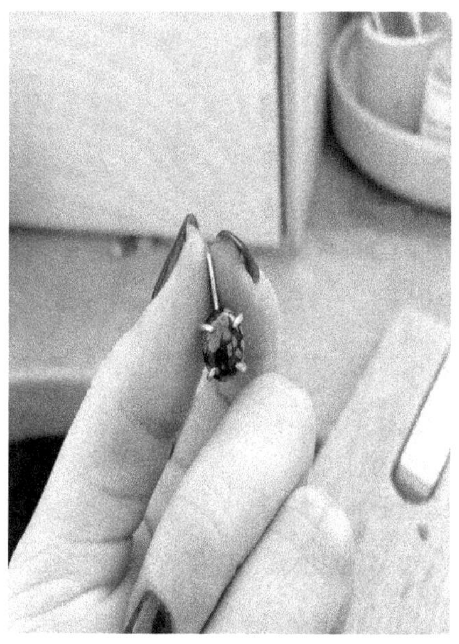

Step eight: Set Stone & Hang on Chain

The very last step is to use your pusher to slowly push every claw over your stone.

``

At this point make use of your finger in your other hand to push against the stone inside the opposite course, allowing you enough resistance to push the claw down completely. Once you have set one claw you ought to then set the claw diagonally across from the stone to 'lock' the stone in region and simplicity the putting of the final two claws. Thread your preferred chain through the bail and rock that piece with pride

CHAPTER FOUR

Steps to make a stunning ring and bracelets (project)

The short cut become to create easy, my friendship wanted one slim ring made with the gold from both jewelry, with the seven 3mm rubies set across the band and a piece of brought granulation detail but She additionally requested a couple of silver big name earrings to be made the usage of the 4mm sapphires from the alternative ring.

I mentioned patterns she favored and I created a board on with inspiration for the ring. I then used these to create a few easy sketches and outlines which I sent to her for comments.

Once she selected a layout she preferred, I labored out the pricing based totally on how long the work become possibly to take and what kind of any more fabric expenses might be. Obviously with remodeling paintings fabric prices are tons decrease but the production fee will be higher as you need to account for the time it takes to rework the metal.

One tip for any bespoke design task hoIver specially for remodeling work is to be very open along with your patron approximately fees. Find out what their budget is at the begin and make sure they may be conscious that there may be greater cloth costs concerned if the metal they offer isn't enough for the redesigned piece.

I generally tend to paintings to an estimate fee with a min-max charge variety for remodeling work because it gives the purchaser a price bracket that they're satisfied with and no danger of nasty surprises when the piece is completed!

One of the rubies becomes a touch too broken so wished replacing and I did a fantastic process of locating the proper stone for the job.

The planning and layout process

Once my purchaser changed into happy with the layout and I had confirmed the info, I started working on cautiously doing away with the stones from the rings. I then Lighted the metallic to see precisely what I needed to be paintings with I had completed this at the first level of dialogue and design hoIver till you put off the stones you cannot determine an exact Light.

I then cut the jewelry into smaller pieces and labored out how a lot gold I might want for every of the stone settings. These have been

``

crafted from little nuggets of gold
which I flattened barely and
would in the end be burned out to
create the seat for the stones.
You can get medical in your
working out how a great deal
steel you want hoIver with
practice you start to judge by way
of eye how a great deal you want
to make a certain size granule!
Once I had made the nuggets for
the settings, I then melted the
ultimate gold and milled into the
proper gauge twine I wished for
the ring shank. Any left-over gold
once the shank became made
become milled once more to
smaller gauge twine and snipped

into portions to make the smaller granules.

Then got here the amusing component: constructing the granulation is my preferred method through far and starting with the primary nugget setting, little by little each granule was soldered into location growing a natural shape, giving the ring a 3-dimensional sense but maintaining it light and comfortable to Iar and I decided to add in a few more silver granules to add evaluation hoIver additionally to maintain charges down. This also allow the precious gold to polish through in place of be buried away under. Once the entirety turned into in region, I then tidied the piece up and burned out the settings equipped for the colossal activity of placing the stones! One of the rubies was a touch too damaged so needed replacing and I did a fabulous task of finding the perfect stone for the process! Before putting any stones, the ring become finished to a very last polish and sent off to the Office for Hallmarking.

One tip for any bespoke layout mission hoIver mainly for remodeling work is to be very open with your purchaser

``

approximately costs. Find out what their finances is at the begin and make certain they're conscious that there can be extra cloth charges concerned if the steel they provide isn't sufficient for the redesigned piece

Processing pictures

The Rings

The authentic rings that belonged
to my hoppy very conventional
9ct gold rings, one with seven

3mm rubies and the opposite with two 4mm sapphires and (three)3cut glass get dressed stones.

Step1: The designs sketching

Initial design sketches, the very last layout evolved from this. I opted for a slimmer 2mm band because the authentic 3mm band proposed would've intended

``

including plenty more gold. It
additionally gave a more delicate
sense to the finished ring.

Step2: Removing & Replacing stone

Carefully putting off the stones without them flying around my workshop and one of the rubies had a small crack and didn't continue to exist being re-set so got here to the rescue with the right replacement.

Step3: The cutting & melting processes

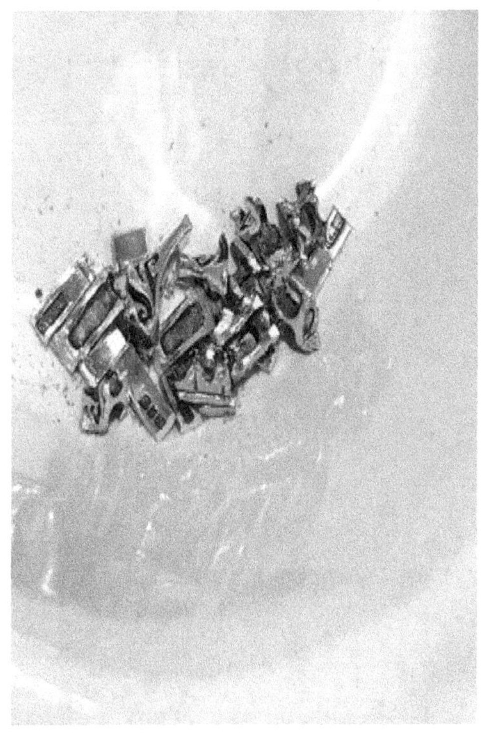

Here the earrings had been then break up equipped for melting I brought another 2g of gold to this after which a few silver for the granules as there wasn't quite sufficient from simply the 2 rings for the whole thing I wanted to acquire within the design.

The shank, nuggets for the settings and a number of the gold granules ready to be pieced collectively. Extra gold and silver granules have been used to fill out the spaces between the settings.

Commencing the placement with the nuggets and granules; this became a sluggish manner as each one was positioned and soldered for my part and once I'd got more than one the settings in place, I ought to then solder necessary of smaller granules without delay and it becomes quite an organic manner and the hoop evolved with every addition of granules.

 Step4: Building and structuring

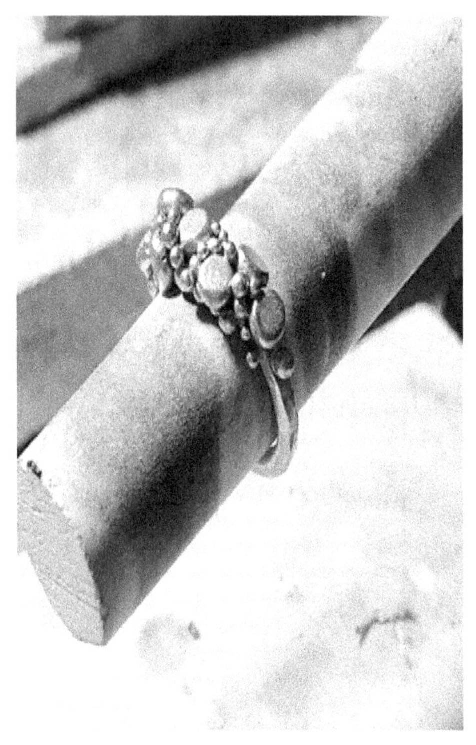

Building the structure and including the very last granules, filling any gaps and ensuring the settings combined in.

Step5: Preparing settings

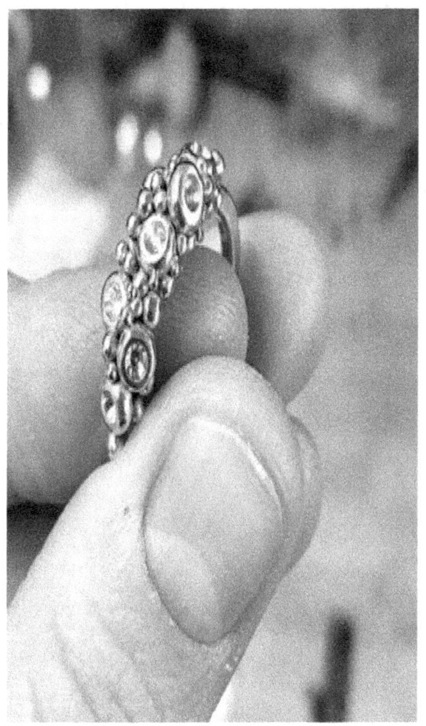

At this point is the cutting the
settings for the rubies and make
sure each setting become cut
individually to fit every stone as
each ruby changed into a slightly

``

exclusive size and form, a few had a Shaw lower intensity and others had a flatter culet which means I couldn't use the 'one size suits all' technique for stone setting.

Step6: Setting of the stones

Testing every ruby's healthy
earlier than placing them one
after the other and be sure each
setting had to be adjusted to in
shape each character stone.

``

Finished Project design

Finally this finishing ring also can be turned into a beautiful stunning bracelet I simply cherished working on this project and there after setting the very last stone I changed into so thrilled to have completed the ring but additionally glad that the task had come to a beautiful bracelet! This fee simply contained a variety of my coronary heart and soul and I felt extremely honored to be asked to create it for my consumer. I became so happy to look the hoop again to its rightful proprietor and turned into over the moon that she changed into so pleased with its transformation.

I had very unique earrings that have been my sister each eternity earrings that I loved hoIver that didn't match me and the fashion of the placing didn't appearance right on me or sit down together with her a beautiful wire wrap wedding ring that I will wear each day which they had keeps in a box for over twenty years.

I began a manner of considering remodeling them in to jewelry that I could Iar masses and that might be something specific and able to be enjoyed in preference to in a drawer. I knew I wanted a new eternity band making with the stones unfold spherical an exclusive sort of band, and initially had notion of having the stones all of the way spherical the brand new ring.

After masses of research, a love of granulation detail and an advice from a chum I met with Zoë. She became capable of translate what changed into in my head into ideas and sketches and advocate at the stone placement to first-rate look after these precious old stones and I decided the stones would be safer all on the front of the ring. I recognize Zoë took remarkable care of the earrings, taking them apart with more special love and attention, I

``

knew they have been in safe fingers.

The result, which turned into an aggregate of all of the gold from the original jewelry together with a little greater and the 7 rubies set with granulation design, was better than I'd ever imagined. It's simply stunning and I cherished the development pictures I received at some stage in the process displaying me its adventure so I knew how it changed into transforming. It genuinely is a one-off particular piece that I now put on proudly all of the time; it has a whole new existence. It receives

``

compliments anywhere I go and

most significantly I suppose my

Grandma would love it, she could

be so pleased it's far now

something lovely worn every day

CHAPTER FIVE

How to make Decorative Ring Setting from Form Cabochon (Project)

Furthermore, creating a bezel putting for an abnormal fashioned stone can appear to be a hard

``

assignment however do not worry, I have given a little by little academic to make it clean for you.

You may want to use this technique on any irregular or unfastened form gemstone of your choice, which includes a boulder opal or a chunk of sea glass you observed on the seashore. The process also can be replicated for calibrated cabochons as properly.

Within this jewelry making guide suggests to you how to create a bezel set ring with a cabochon. This is the sort of beautiful statement ring, with that suitable

pop of coloration and I hope it
facilitates you find a few thought
in your subsequent project!

The strategies within this jewelry making educational can be used to create a layout with greater element or something that is easy to fit your taste and logo. Take a study the bottom of this chapter for notion the use of unfastened form stones.

Project Tools & materials require:

- Your selected cabochon

- Bench peg & anvil

- Bezel strip

- Silver sheet zero.5mm used in this undertaking

- Beaded cord 1.5mm used in this project

``

- Metal cutters; saw body, noticed blades & beeswax

- Files

- Scriber

- Solder paste and needle

- Soldering block

- Third hand

- Gas torch

- Pickle

- TIezers

- Plastic tweezers

- Quench bowl & water

- It and dry sanding sheets

- Bezel rocker or pusher

- Burnisher

- Polishing papers, strength device consisting of Dremel 4000 Multi Tool with silicone polishers or barreling device

- Ring mandrel

Step 1: Measure Bezel Strip

Now begin via measuring the
depth of your chosen stone and
select the right bezel strip
duration. The idea is to have
simply sufficient bezel to push

over the stone all through setting, so that you can ensure the beauty of the stone isn't hidden by means of an excessive amount of bezel!

Any place the stone starts off evolved to dome, is the height in which you want the bezel.

This is hard on a free-form stone as they can be abnormal but bear in mind that the putting may be adjusted once the bezel is in region.

Step 2: Cut Bezel

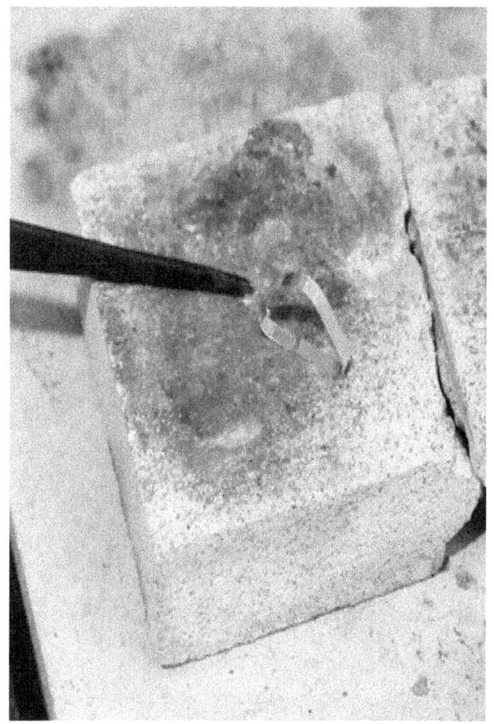

In next wrap the bezel strip across the stone and use a scriber to mark on the strip wherein you will need to cut.

Always try to have the join on the straightest phase of the stone for ease and use the brink of the bezel strip as a manual as this will come up with matching ends; having ends that in shape perfectly will make it less difficult so as to solder them together.

Use your files to create a neat flushed be part of if the ends are not perfectly aligned.

Step 3: Soldering and Pickle

Before you solder the bezel strip check that you stone fits snuggly in the placing and that the ends definitely meet.

Flux the be part of solder paste already has flux included in it so

``

there may be no need to flux if the use of this and use difficult solder paste or pallions to solder the ends together after which quench and pickle your piece to cast off hearth stain. Remove from the pickle after a few minutes and inspect thebe a part of it.

File and smooth up to be part of the use of documents and wet and dry papers.

Step four: Attaching bezel to the metal sheet

``

At this point make use of a jewelry saw to cut the desired quantity of steel sheet wished for the layout. Now it's time to area the bezel at the silver sheet that you are using and use medium solder to join them collectively.

The bezel ought to contact the sheet all of the manner round and there ought to be no gaps. Flux the location if using pallions where you'll solder the bezel onto the silver sheet, area solder at the internal of the bezel then vicinity onto your layout. Solder the two together, then quench and pickle.

Step 5: Trim metal sheet

Using jewelry snips reduce the extra metal sheet and report clean, leaving a 2mm gap round the edge so you can add some beaded wire to the layout.

Step 6: Wrap Beaded Wire jewelry

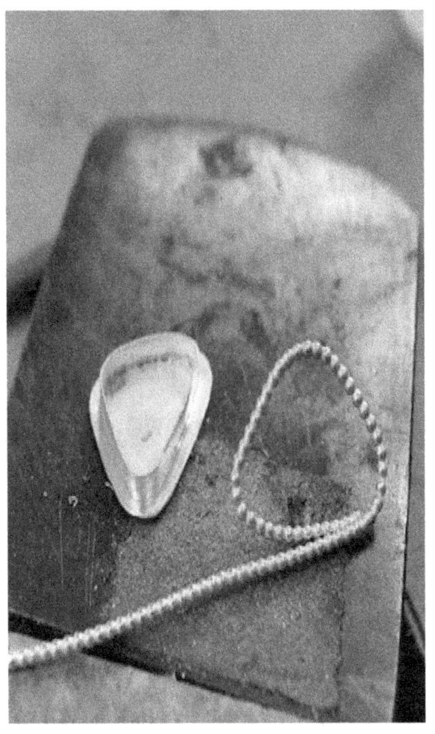

Next wrap the setting with the beaded cord right here I have used 1.5mm, reduce the amount you want the usage of your saw
``

and make certain that the cord touches on the ends.

Using smooth solder and the equal soldering strategies stated in the previous steps are part of the beaded cord to the placing at the 2mm segment that surrounds the bezel placing.

Step 7: Create Ring Band Jewelry

Next make a simple ring band the usage of a hoop length guide and the following calculation to get the suitable length - calculation: diameter x pi three.14 + thickness of steel.

Once you've got worked out an appropriate period which you need, mark it on the twine.

At this degree reduce greater cord than what you need so that the ends overlap next to every different, so that you can use a saw to reduce thru each ends at the marked period this manner you may have ends that match flawlessly together. Follow my grade by grade teaching guide on how to make a hoop band here.

Using the solder techniques referred to in the preceding stages; solder the ring collectively with smooth solder, quench and pickle.

``

Step 8: Solder Together and Pickle

Remove the hoop from the pickle
and shape it on a hoop mandrel,
remembering to show the ring

over at the mandrel for an even shape.

File the threshold of the ring where the putting will take a seat so that it's far flat this may make it less complicated to solder the 2 flat portions collectively.

Place the bezel setting the wrong way up on a soldering block and using a third hand, area the hoop with the flat area down onto the setting and line it up centrally. Solder the two portions together using smooth solder. Quench and pickle the piece.

Step 9: Polishing stage

Clean up your design using files,

It & dry papers, sharpening

papers/silicon polishers and at

this factor check the intensity of

the bezel putting in opposition to

your stone.

Lay dental tape throughout the putting in order that the stone may be effortlessly eliminated after checking the intensity, this can ensure you're happy with the intensity.

Once the stone is within the placing, it will be tough to get it out again. The purpose is to have the minimum quantity of bezel protruding above the stone, in order that whilst you push the bezel side over it you may not be hiding it. If the height of the bezel desires lowering and you could use your files to do this, you could also reduce the thickness of the bezel as this will

``

make it less difficult to push or rub over.

Step 10: Push Bezel over Stone

Using your pusher or bezel rocker gently push the bezel over the stone in a downward movement and be very careful no longer to touch the stone specifically if it's

``

far a smooth or an opal as you may mark the pinnacle of it.

Start at an awkward phase after which circulate across the stone, every time pushing in the opposite path to the phase you've got simply done, until you've got driven the bezel over the stone all the manner round.

Step 11: Burnish stage

Continue to do that till you have a smooth end this is flush towards the stone.

Use a burnishes at the segment of the bezel you have got just driven or rubbed over, to provide it a high polished look.

CHAPTER SIX

How to set Gemstones in Backset Settings Jewelry (project)

Backset settings are a brief and clean way to set faceted

``

gemstones while jewelry making. They may be integrated into necklaces, bracelets and rings to make lovely gemstone jewelry and simply pop on your desire of gemstone then fold the claws over the again the use of a couple of tweezers. I deliver those easy to use settings in both sterling silver and 9ct gold and in a variety of sizes, as Ill as in equipped to go earrings. They are furnished without stones so you can pick your favored from our variety of faceted gem stones to go along with the layout you've got in thoughts.

Tools wished in project

A pair of tweezers, pliers or comparable

Follow my little by little commands with pix guide to show how to set your gemstone in a backset placing.

How to Set Backset Settings

Step 1:

Select your backset setting and matching sized faceted gemstone and in this project I have used an 8x6mm oval slide pendant set with an 8x6mm oval iolite faceted stone.

Step 2:

Place the faceted gemstone flat side down into the putting as proven.

``

Step three:

Push down every of the metal
claws over the again of the stone
so that the gemstone is held
securely in location and you can
use a pair of tweezers, pliers or
similar and I will also advise you

``

to be pushing opposite claws one after the alternative to ensure the stone is precisely vital.

Step 4:

Your backset putting is now whole! Backset settings create fashionable and traditional looking jewelry designs and open

up a whole array of viable
thoughts.

Cubic Zirconium Backset Earring
Kit

``

Pink Quartz Earrings

Silver Sapphire Necklace

Cornflower Blue Sapphire

Necklace

Shop my complete variety of jewelry settings eBook for faceted stones to make lovely pieces of jewelry.

Great for jewelry making novices, I've a brilliant variety of prepared-made settings including rings, earrings and pendants wherein you need minimum equipment to set your stones. I additionally have loose and mount for faceted stones, where you can thread wire, glue or solder onto your designs.

CHAPTER SEVEN

How to Work Harden Jewelry Making Wire

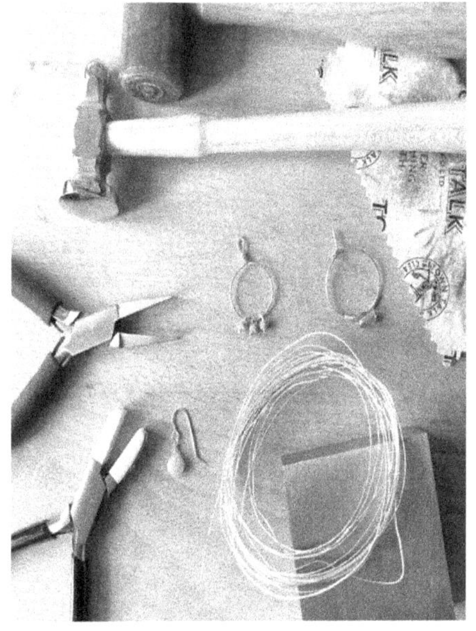

I share with you simple methods you may work harden metal cord in your jewelry designs. Get all the tools and substances online with a guide.

``

What is painting hardening?

Work hardening in jewelry making is the process of changing the temper of the cord to make the cord stronger.

Why you need to work harden your wire

Metal jewelry cord is available in a variety of hardness and gentle, 1/2 difficult and tough. When using smooth twine as an instance, you will locate that it is sincerely easy to bend out of form which means you need to paintings harden it is withstand your selected design and ensure it does not lose its shape.

Undoing work hardening wire

Although it's not virtually essential for twine wrapping strategies, you may undo work hardening by way of the process of annealing. This is heating the cord to a sure temperature so one can soften it and make it malleable once more.

Can you work harden too much?

Yeah! Be conscious that work hardening metal cord an excessive amount of can make it brittle and can reason it to snap. Always maintain trying out your cord for the duration of the technique of labor hardening to ensure it isn't being worked on extra than vital and if you really discover that the cord is on the brink of breaking, you may anneal it to avoid this from taking place.

Do I have to work hardened earlier than beginning my layout?

This relies upon on your preferred layout hoIver if you could; it is endorsed to start paintings hardening before developing your design. Be cautious in case you are work hardening afterward, in particular when you have added gemstones as you do not want to hazard unfavorable them.

Steel you can you work harden

You can paintings harden maximum jewelry making cord which includes silver, brass, copper and gold. I would propose

``

performing some research in case you plan on the usage of another metallic earlier than going in advance.

Shop jewelry making cord

Explore our variety of jewelry making twine to fit your wishes from sterling silver, eco-friendly, 9ct gold, copper and brass. Our sterling silver and 9ct gold cord is furnished gentle completely annealed, and our copper and brass is half of tough.

Our sterling silver, green silver cord and 9ct gold wire can be reduce to the size that fits you.

``

THANK YOU FOR READING

* 9 7 9 8 7 2 6 6 2 5 5 8 4 *